# The Future of Multi-level Marketing in Europe

*To Keith and Jacky,*

*I hope that this book will help you to present your wonderful opportunity.*

*Kind Regards,*

*Paul Kumunche*

*Newcastle, Sept 10, 1996*

Original Title
"L'avenir de la vente multi-niveaux en Europe"
© Les Editions du Saint-Bernard

Translated by Janet V. Alover

Printed in Belgium

Les Editions du Saint-Bernard
278, avenue Coghen
B-1180 BRUXELLES

ISBN: 2-9600090-1-0
Dépot Légal en Belgique: Juin 1995-D/1995/7252/2

All rights of translation and reproduction for all countries. Apart from any fair dealing for the purposes of research or private study, or criticism or review, this publication may not be reproduced by any means, photography, repro graphic reproduction, unless with the prior permission in writing of the publishers. Belgian author's rights Act, 31 July 1994 shall be applicable in case of tort, including the penalties.

Paul Dewandre
Corinne Mahieu

# The Future of Multi-level Marketing In Europe

*Editions
du Saint Bernard*

*Acknowledgement*
*We would like to thank Keith Hunniford*
*for his help in adapting this English version of our book*

# Preface

*When a friend invited us to a Multi-level Marketing opportunity meeting in January 1992, what we heard interested us greatly.*

*This type of marketing is not new. It has existed for many years already, but it is, they said, the opportunity of the decade. And we were there at the right time.*

*We asked ourselves why would this distribution method, which had been used so little in the past now develop with such great success?*

*We have studied financial reports on the Multi-level Marketing industry and have noticed that some companies using this technique have really shown un usual growth.*

*But does this growth alone prove that Multi-level Marketing will develop in the future to the point where in ten years time it will be a popular means of distribution?*

*This book contains our reflections on these issues.*

*We hope that it will help people answer their own questions.*

Le Trayas, February 1995

# Multi-level Marketing: Short term fad or long term trend?

We are going through a period of economic and social evolution. Our work environment is changing and the media speak of economic crisis.

While numerous enterprises are making people redundent and others are filing for bankruptcy, new companies are born everyday. Some have seen surprising growth figures and realised great profits.

Product innovation has for many companies resulted in a business boom. Such breakthroughs can take several forms.

One is the development of a new product. The Walk Man invented by Sony, brought the company incredible revenues.

Alternatively, one can achieve the competitive edge through a technological improvement in a product. The CD is a good example. When it became popular, the vinyl record industry disappeared overnight. While companies that made vinyl records had to lay-off their personnel and close their doors, the manufacturers of CDs have prospered.

Innovations in production itself have allowed a number of manufacturing firms to reduce the costs of making their product. The automation of production lines assures a higher return and permits these firms to have greater profits.

Another form of innovation is a change in location of the production site. Delocalising has permitted numerous firms to diminish production costs. Finding the labels "Made in China" or "Made in Taiwan" no longer surprises anyone. Production costs are lower in regions where manhours and warehousing are less expensive. Transportation costs have also gone down greatly in the last few years, therefore making it possible to manufacture quality products abroad at a better price.

Another innovation involves in product distribution. It is even commonly recognised that innovations in this area today constitute one of the major challenges for commerce in Europe. We see new means of distribution developing - such as mail order, TV home shopping, direct selling, and the minitel selling now available in France. Firms look for better ways to serve their clients.

A distribution technique that more and more people are talking about is Multi-level Marketing or MLM, also called network marketing. This distribution method appeared for the first time in the 1940's in the United States.

For the last ten years, in the United States and in Japan, the turnover of some firms using MLM has skyrocketed. The number of companies including this form of distribution as part of their strategy goes up every year.

Similarly the increase in turnover of MLM firms shows the success of independent distributors who have generated them. Some American MLM distributors have created networks so large that in only five years they can now retire.

In recent years, this trend has been evident in Europe also. Some countries such as Great Britain and Germany, already boast large MLM networks whereas other countries, like France and Spain, have felt the effects of this movement much more recently.

People either love MLM or they hate it. While some newspapers and television stations scream scandal, opportunity meetings are springing up all over our area.

We are often torn between two emotions when we first come in contact with MLM. A great enthusiasm: "Yes! this is exactly what I want to do. It seems fun, lucrative, and simple", but, when after sharing this enthusiasm with a friend, mother, or spouse, warning signals start to flash : "That's an illegal pyramid! It's a sect! You are going to get cleaned out!"

What does one make of this?

Can MLM develop in our marketplace as it has in the United States and Japan? Is it a real opportunity or a fad that is going to fade out just as quickly as it appeared?

How does this distribution method compare to other means of distribution that are also developing — such as direct selling, mail order, and TV home shopping?

Are criticisms based on ethical principles? Do they seek to protect the consumer from poor quality products, or the distributor from himself? Or maybe the detractors voice is simply a classic resistance often encountered at the beginning of any change? Are these dismissals not founded on fear of the unknown — a fear caused by lack of information?

Can we predict the future of this type of business? Is it reasonable to think that MLM will soon be as well known in Europe as the franchise? Are MLM distributors visionaries, pioneers, or madmen?

There are answers to these questions. Even if we can not predict the future with certainty, we can see that the trends of tomorrow are taking shape today. If we analyse these trends which mark our daily lives and compare them to the principles by which MLM functions we can decide whether or not MLM will suit our new working and purchasing habits.

In order to see the future of MLM, we must answer the following questions:

— What are the European trends of tomorrow?
— By what principles does MLM work?
— Does MLM match the tomorrow's trends

\*

# Part One

# What does the future hold?

*To predict is difficult, especially the future.*
Pierre Dac

# Chapter I
# Knowing the Trends of Tomorrow

Is there a formula for predicting the future? This question must be answered by every firm that wants to innovate. If it wants to create a new product, will consumers like it? Will a new packaging please them more? Will a different form of publicity have more impact?

*"No one knows (exactly) how the future will feel or unfold, but the trends are taking us there with a force that's almost tangible"* writes Faith Popcorn in her *Popcorn Report*.[1]

Every day we are confronted by an incalculable amount of information from a wide variety of sources: television, radio, advertisements, newspapers, books, journals, shop windows, fashion in the street, the new architecture of buildings, new cars, conversations that we have or have overheard, etc.

---

[1] Faith Popcorn, *The Popcorn Report* (Reading: Arrow, 1991) 131.

We record this information subconsciously and hardly pay attention to it, but we can also regroup, dissect, analyse, compare, and discern general trends from it.

The 1950's was typified by cars with chrome bumpers, the modern kitchen, nylon, and the Juke Box . . . the 1960's saw feminism, the Beatles, the pill changed morals, and the miniskirt created a uproar. . . In the 1970's we had hippies, the petrol crisis, bohemianism and communal life. The 1980's represented the me-cult, the Sloan ranger, aerobics, computers, and being "plugged-in.", . . .

**The nineties**

The trends of today are more difficult to define. The lack of hindsight makes the exercise less easy, but words like environment, cocooning, nature, technology, bio, purity and ethics appear to be the most characteristic of our time.

Some futurologists have studied the question in depth with interesting conclusions.

Faith Popcorn founded and directs a company called Brainreserve[2]. It is an American firm of marketing consultants with a worldwide reputation. The company's nickname is "The Nostradamus of Marketing." A majority of the giants of industry: Coca Cola, Gillette, Toyota, Martini, and AT&T are among its clients and swear by its method of "analysis of the conformity to trends."

Faith Popcorn and her team have used a method called "brainstorming" to identify ten major trends that mark daily life in the United States[3].

---

[2] See her *Popcorn Report* cited above

[3] They are listed in Appendix 1 of this book

For the last fifteen years, another American, John Naisbitt, has published a Trend Report that sells for $15,000 a copy.[4] From analysis of the written and televised press, and the frequency of themes that have been in the news, the Naisbitt group has defined the *Megatrends* that influence our macro-economy.[5]

It is generally accepted that Europe follows, but lags behind American trends. European mentality, however, is not always the same as it is in the United States. Our "old world" culture has its own characteristics and richness.

European studies on this topic help us by giving an insight into these issues.[6]

By using the same techniques as American futurologists, we can formulate a list of the six most important European trends that will be predominant in the coming years.

\*

---

[4] John Naisbitt, *Megatrends* (New York: Warner, 1982) and *Megatrends 2000* (New York: Avon, 1990).

[5] A summary-listing of the Naisbitt group's *Megatrends* is found in Appendix 2 of this book.

[6] As Credoc in France and Statistisches Bundesamt in Germany.

## The First Trend: The Return Home

The most important trend of our decade is "The Return Home". It began in the 1980's.

Faith Popcorn uses the word "cocoon" to describe this trend. She predicted as early as 1970 that Americans would retreat to the safety and comfort of their homes and park themselves in their easy-chairs with a remote control in hand and telephone close by to order pizzas.

This has not only been seen to happen in the United States, but has stretched internationally, even as far as Japan and Western Europe.

All of a sudden we think that discos are old news! Now we want to relax in a hot bath after a long days work, followed by a cozy evening of conversation at home. We order a take away, or choose a preprepared meal out of the freezer and heat it in the microwave then watch a video that has just been delivered by motorcycle. The services that come to the home even include hairstylists and car washing. A pressing service comes to take suits and bring them back the next day, and banks offer telephone services.

We think twice before we put on a coat to fight daily traffic jams, the danger of the streets, noise, smoke-filled restaurants, overworked waiters, and parking spaces which are difficult to find.

We enjoy the company of our children,and pets, settle into our new station wagon, and set off to take a long walk in the woods on a Sunday. The "cocoon home" has extended to the "cocoon car". Forward air-bags and side protection comfort us with the idea of cushioned security.

## The Second Trend: The Wary Buyer

Thoughtless, reckless money spending is now part of the distant past. We demand quality at a reasonable price. We read labels down to the fine print and scrutinise deceptive publicity. We have become adult consumers.

We buy consumer magazines and read comparative tests, then maybe buy another one to compare results or ask the opinions of those around us. Are the results from magazines corroborated by our friends' opinions? Television programs also interest "The Wary Buyer." It is increasingly common to find informational programs taking up prime time TV slots.

When we do buy we want an after-sales warranty and will only buy from a supplier we have confidence in. For this reason companies are setting up systems of free phone help lines to inform their clients about the quality and origin of their products.

\*

## The Third Trend: Personalised Selling

In today's market we demand "Personalised Selling" to meet our own unique and specific expectations. We claim our right to be different and to have our own identity. We no longer want uniformity, but customised service.

"*Today customers come first.*" writes Denis Waitley.[7]

---

[7] Denis Waitley, *Empires of the Mind* (London: Nicholas Brealey Publishing, 1995) 2.

Whereas in the past we may have chosen a piece of furniture based purely on its aesthetics we now enjoy having the option to select individual upholstery, choose dimensions to suit our personal needs, etc.

When we buy a car, we can choose the interior fabric and the exterior paint from a wide selection. Then we choose options: with air conditioning and ABS, without central locking, etc. Customised options for our rolling cocoon !

Today, product quality is of primary importance. We don't want to buy poor quality, or merchandise that won't last. We demand solidity, beauty, and perfection.

Service is just as important. We choose our suppliers not only by the quality of their products but also by the services that accompany the sale, both during and after. We like to be recognised by our suppliers. A little birthday card, or a personalised letter in respect to our tastes and habits makes a big difference. Peugeot has created a repair service for emergency break-downs, for their vehicles as well as for others in several European countries. It is often the extra services that help us choose between one manufacturer and another.

*

## **The Fourth Trend: Nature and technology**

Our crazy race to success is poisoning us. The constant 'rush to the office and back home to bed' has made many throw in the towel. In the 1970's people started to think about going back to a healthier lifestyle.

Some even went as far as leaving behind their suits and fancy jobs to leave and raise sheep in the hills.[8]

But this was limited by a lack of technology. It was hard to make a living selling cheese and to advertise a farm that had been turned into a bed and breakfast. . .

Then the technological innovations of the computing age started to impact our lives. Fax, PC, better telephone services, cheap air-travel, motorways — all of these make the world a smaller place and are invaluable to the entrepreneur.

With them it is now possible to keep in touch with business without always having to be in the dowtown office.

So what keeps people in the city? Work, school, cultural attractions — but these in time will all be accessible from the home. Couples often dream of working together from their own home. Mothers regret not being able to take care of their young kids at home. Technology can improve the "Quality of Life" and grey the distinction between home and work place.

Telephone services including conference-calling will improve in the next few years and costs will go down. It is reasonable to expect that in five years time most systems will send visual images as well as sound and we will be able to have face to face telephone conversations.

Soon families will be able to live in the country and still receive a full education. Children from several neighbouring families will get together to watch school by video-conference. Having been raised on Nintendo and interactive laser-disc, this will seem quite normal to them.

---

[8] See, in France, Danièle Léger et Bertrand Hervieu, *Le retour à la nature*, (Paris: Seuil, 1979).

Should we then be afraid that human contacts will disappear? Just ask anybody who lives in a city and who has spent time in the country, or anybody who lives in the country who has spent time in the city. Can we really say that human relationships in the city are "warm"? Have we made unforgettable acquaintances while waiting in traffic jams or on the underground? Neighbourly readiness to lend a helping hand is legendary in villages, yet we barely even say 'hello' to the person living in the flat next door.

In large cities such as in Paris and Berlin, 50% of households comprise of only one occupant and there are innumerable divorces caused by lack of communication. Do these people experience a quality of life and feel part of a community?

*

## **The Fifth Trend**: The Quality of Life

Parallel to the trend to retreat from a hectic life, we no longer want to, nor can be, employed in the same job by the same employer until the end of our days. In the 1960's, we studied and went to work for a large company. It was so easy! Our place was guaranteed. The movie *The Laureate*, starring Dustin Hoffman, retells the dilemma of the period: *"I am worrying about my future"* says the young man. *"Plastics"* his uncle responds. The solution in one word.

What does life in a company now offer us? Good pay, certainly, but at what price? We are often tied down by the stress of work hours that we can not choose, offers and refusals of promotions and pay increase. We no longer enjoy our free time because we only use it to relax from the tiring life that we lead. We would love to spend more time with our family and give more time to wondering whether or not this crazy race is really worth the effort.

For some of us, the race ends abruptly. We are laid-off and begin the even more depressing task of finding a new job. The "new unemployed" are engulfed in deep depression. The tacit contract that binds us to our firms — "I give you my time, you give me the security to know that I will still be paid tomorrow" — is no longer renewed. Companies have had to realise that it is no longer economically feasible to keep on personnel "for better or for worse."

We no longer want to feel like we are on the verge of this sort of catastrophe. The best way to avoid it is to create our own business. No more fixed work hours, no more nasty rivalry with a colleague for the same coveted position.

*"So who will be left behind in the traditional corporate structure? Who knows?"* asks Faith Popcorn. *"The insecure, maybe, and the meanest."*[9]

To work for oneself does not mean to work less. On the contrary, the self-employed are often more relentless and dynamic, but they do control their own lives. They put their future in their own hands.

\*

---

[9] See *Popcorn Report*, quoted above, 55.

We are fed up of being dependent on hand-outs. We can no longer count on the government to pamper us. The welfare state no longer gives anything but false hopes. Is there no one to protect us? We can protect ourselves. We have already begun to do this in relation to our health. We believe less in medicine that is guaranteed to cure everything miraculously. We now make the first step on our own by paying more attention to the quality of our lives, eating better and exercising regularly.

The advice of experts is no longer the "holy word." We have read a large part of what interests us from specialised magazines and from in-depth studies. Works that explain scientific discoveries in common terms are readily available. Magazines for the general public contain pointed articles about medical and scientific discoveries and the most recent philosophical research... We are our own experts.

We have reclaimed a new physical and moral health and want to believe in ourselves. We now know that we need to work on our subconscious to overcome our limitations. Yesterday, only crazy people went to see the psychiatrist. Today healthy people consult a psychoanalyst, a psychologist, a group or relationship therapist without hesitation. We no longer fear letting our desire for a better state of mental health be known. Works on psychology and personal development sell easily in the corner shop!

Companies, one after another, have started to organise personal development seminars. The original idea was to improve employee relationships in order to achieve the best possible communication between team members. The demand for training has increased so dramatically that a new industry of qualified consultants has developed to supply this niche market. The most common trainings involve goal setting and time management, but other areas include public speaking, self confidence, memory skills, and team work. These sort of trainings have now become so popular that more and more people are taking them on their own initiative.

We have realised in the last few years that we have forgotten some fundamentally important things. Money is no longer of primary importance. The quality of the relationships with those around us — both at home and at work — is an increasingly high priority. We want a full life that is happy and healthy.

*

### **The Sixth Trend**: A search for ethics

"*Yesterday profits were earned through expediency. Today profits are earned with integrity.*" writes Denis Waitley.[10]

We want to reclaim our values. We buy products that respect the environment or that are made by manufacturers who support humanitarian causes. We look for sincere products — ones that give us the feeling of being a "moral" consumer.

The search for profit has its limits. We feel as though we have been tricked by greedy politicians and business people who have money and power. Our leaders are now having to make their actions known to the nation. Transparency has replaced corruption and governments can not afford to break the rules anymore.

---

[10] Denis Waitley, *Empires of the Mind* (London: Nicholas Breatley Publishing, 1995) 2.

Certainly we have to do something that allows us to put money in the bank, but we also want to do something honourable. It is no longer fashionable to succeed at the expense of others.

We look for real relationships based on respect for one another. *"Liberal socialism,"* Naisbitt says : we will pass "from being the helped out, to the individual making it on his own," a time which will be marked by *"the triumph of the individual."*[11]

∗

---

[11] See Naisbitt's *Megatrends* and *Megatrends 2000* which are summarised in Appendix 2 of this book.

# Chapter II
# The Consequences of These Trends

These trends manifest themselves in everyday life, but for the most part, they influence two facets of our environment: we are changing our *buying* and *working* habits.

## New buying habits

Companies have to adapt to our new requirements. We do not want to run around in the shops anymore. Let them come to us! Catalogues, telephone, television, a passing friend — allow us to select what we like quietly and at home.

Small stores do not fulfil tomorrow's trends. Finding a parking place, lugging around purchases, doing the round of all of the stores. . . We still have to do this sometimes, but we no longer like to do our shopping like this. It is much easier to pick up the phone and give our credit card number.

Large stores do not fulfil tomorrow trends either. Harsh lighting, shopping cart crashes — this does not match with our desire to "Return Home". Long lines at the check-out, cashiers who would rather talk amongst themselves than to the client, and who do not even say "hello" — this does not correspond to our desire for "Personalised Selling." It is all anti "custom-made". The biggest, modern grocery stores have begun to respond to our expectations. Customer service is getting better. Personalised convenience charge cards and plans are appearing, as are specialised food sections and catering services.

We still go to the grocery shop regularly. It is a way to save time and the only way to stock up on what we need, but how long will we continue to go there? Only until another way to grocery shop is available — one more suited to our desires. There are already some companies that do the shopping for you and home-deliver. Some stores make catalogues of their merchandise, take your order by phone, and send out your choice by mail. This will get more popular. Faith Popcorn thinks that we will only go to grocery stores for the fun of it from time to time, since grocery stores will still be the centre of other attractions, like the bustling of daily life, games, and taste-testing of new foods.[12]

The suppliers of goods must find a way to serve us at home, know us personally, serve us more affably, and to guarantee an unquestionable after-sale service.

In fact, such ways do exist and are already used by a growing number of companies.

## Non store retailing

Generally under the term non store retailing are grouped all sorts of alternative types of purchasing like direct selling and distance selling.

---
[12] Faith Popcorn, 166.

These alternative means of distribution have already developed.[13] They permit a more personal approach to selling. Direct selling, mail order, TV home shopping, and MLM have lately seen phenomenal growth.

## Direct selling

Direct selling can either be one-to-one between a representative and client in their home or in the form of a product party or showcase. Many companies operate in Europe with travelling salespeople on either a salaried or independent basis, who offer goods and services to consumers. The personalised contact and service that the salesperson provides the client meets the demands of the European market.

## Mail order

Another form of non store retailing is mail order. The client purchases from home something they have seen in a catalogue, an advertisement in the press or a mail shot. Orders are then placed by mail or telephone and delivered, often by the regular post, but sometimes by a service maintained by the mail order company.

This type of selling is not new, but it is getting more and more popular in Europe.

Mail order conforms also to trends such as "The Return Home" and "Personalised Selling". Abiding to this latter trend, some mail order companies distribute the

---

[13] In Germany, up to 23 % of all goods are already bought outside of a traditional store. See Prof. Dr Engelhart, *Definition and volume of direct selling of goods and service to Consumers,* (Ruhr University of Bochum, Germany : unplished).

same catalogue under different names to capture a wider target market. Mail order also conforms to the trend of "The Wary Buyer" who takes time to choose and compare, knowing they can change their mind and return the product if they want to.

Nowadays mail order companies use the most recent technological innovations at their disposal: automated wrapping systems, perfected computer networks, the French minitel, and voice-mail systems to optimise their efficiency.

**TV home shopping**

The first TV home shopping programs were broadcast in Italy in 1974. They have been a success ever since.

In 1985 similar programs in the United States resulted in a national network broadcasting TV home shopping twenty-four hours a day. We look forward to the arrival of these American TV home shopping companies to the European market. The broadening of the TV cable has contributed to its success.

There exist other types of catalogues which television also has at its disposal such as video-catalogues which permit the selection of merchandise with the aid of a VCR. They have not yet found a wide circulation, but the development of the video-disc allowing a clearly focused picture to be stopped momentarily, will probably bring about a decisive break-through.

**Multi-level marketing**

MLM constitutes the most recent sort of direct selling. The basic principle is that a large number of people carry out a few individual sales each. Distributors advertise the product and are compensated accordingly by the manufacturer. The consumer benefits from the advice of a friend and an in-home selling service.

This method of distribution and its principles are analysed in further detail in the second part of the book.

From the consumer's point of view, MLM offers a new means of buying that corresponds to the trends of "Return to Home", "Personalised Selling", and "The Wary Buyer", but this industry also permits those who wish, to start their own distribution companies.

Does it correspond to our new working habits as well?

\*

## The new working habits

All of our working habits have changed. Working for large companies corresponds less and less to our desire to spend more time cocooned at home, have control of our lives and feel more fulfilled.

What impact does this have today?

Paul Pilzer writes that in 1931 a young English student won a scholarship to study in the United States.[14] He was surprised to find that in a country known for its business opportunities, the large part of Americans preferred to work in large companies rather than as individual business people.

---

[14] Paul Zane Pilzer and Mark and Renee Reid Yarnell, *Should You Quit Before You're Fired?* (Carson City, Nevada: Quantum Leap, 1992) 39-41

*"Why, in a free market economy, would a worker voluntarily submit to direction by a corporation instead of selling his own output or service directly to customers in the market."*[15]

The student was Ronald Coase, who won a Nobel Prize in economics in 1991. His work of 1931, *The Nature of the Firm*, analyses the reasons why people stay in large companies.

Even after 60 years, this work is still one of the most frequently cited in contemporary economic research. Professor Pilzer thinks that if Coase studied the same subject today, however, he would come to diametrically opposite conclusions.

In *The Nature of the Firm*, Ronald Coase explains the success of large firms in terms of their ability to reduce 'transaction costs' between individuals. He cites an example in which a manager wants to dictate a letter and have it typed. The manager could hire someone for the specific task of typing the letter, but the transaction cost of hiring such an employee for a set time would greatly exceed the value of the work demanded. Looking for a secretary, assessing their abilities, and negotiating a salary would all be an unnecessary waste of time for the manager who finally decides to type the letter himself.

The interest of large firms has been to reduce transactions costs between themselves and the suppliers who provide services by hiring people with the necesssary skills on a permanent basis. This diminishes the number of contract negotiations. Labour contracts are only discussed at the moment of hire and later, for possible pay-

---

[15] Paul ZanePilzer, 44 as cited from «Ronald Harry Coase,» *The New Palgrave: A Dictionary of Economics* (London: Macmillian, 1987) 455.

raises. Unfortunately the firm looses its work flexibility. The company has the advantage that there is always someone available to perform each task yet at the same time it risks not being able to occupy the employee if there is a work slowdown. The employees themselves loose their independence and the ability to manage their own time, in exchange for a regular salary and a stable position.

Meanwhile as the company grows it generates expenses in the management of personnel. The larger the company gets the more difficult it is to transmit information through, which will result in bad decisions making and consequently increased costs. In addition are the costs of laying-off personnel. These have risen enormously with the growth in the protection of workers' rights. Coase named all of these costs "inefficiency costs".

For Coase, a firm is the ideal size when the transaction costs are equal to the inefficiency costs, but since 1930, the drop in transaction costs has been proportional to the rise in inefficiency costs.

Indeed, transaction costs that are added to goods and services furnished by a supplier outside the company (i.e. the cost of communication, delivery and accounting) have become so low in respect to the value of the goods and services that it is often no longer considered when selecting a supplier. Likewise transaction costs — telephone and fax - will decrease even more in the future.

Inefficiency costs, however, have become a major burden to large firms. Since the 1960's, due to inflation that began in that period, employees have become accustomed to receiving annual pay rises that are independent of their individual job performance.

It is no longer unusual to hear of a situation where two employees in a large firm carry out exactly the same job. One has just been hired, and the other has ten years seniority. Even if the final result of their work is exactly the same, their pay may vary by as much as 50%.

The cost of workers in terms of taxes, social security payments, and pension funds are a considerable burden to business. They also increase regularly regardless of the workers' performance.

But according to Coase, the main reason for increases in inefficiency costs in large companies is their inability to quickly apply new technologies and evolve to suit changing needs. The entrepreneur on the other hand can gain the competitive edge as they are flexible enough to avoid these problems.

At the start of the computing age it was only the large corporations who had the resources for leading edge technologies. Now every small business can afford the latest computers.

Likewise, in the past only employees of these large companies had the opportunity to work with new technologies. Today, the key to success, for both companies and individuals, is to learn to use technology as soon as it is available. Only the ability to adapt to innovation will allow people to pull themselves out of economic crisis. Employees of large firms who are known more for their fidelity than for their ability to innovate are usually the last to learn new skills.

When an employee joins a company they first go through a period of training. What they learn during this period makes them more of an asset. Following this initiation period, over time they may receive promotion and consequently an increase in salary. If there comes a time when their value to the company does not increase, yet they still receive pay rises, they can evaluate the situation for themselves. Two risks await: either unemployment or the company's bankruptcy!

If the resistance to change of the less dynamic employees in a company results in the slow implementation of new technologies, the more dynamic element will look to escape from the limits being imposed upon them. They are going to give up less and less of their liberty in exchange for promises of job security that are no longer fulfilled. Setting up their own business is a dream shared by an increasing number of people.

The corporate system is not, however, going to fall apart overnight. It still offers many advantages to employers and employees alike. It is obvious that some companies will adapt to technological changes and will avoid inefficiency costs by selecting a restricted number of the most dynamic and open-minded candidates from the job market.

According to Faith Popcorn, we will witness a complete transformation in the structure of work:

*"Future teams of workers can still meet for conferences and lunches, or gossip-and-coffee sessions over the telescreen. The corporate headquarters, though smaller, can still exist, to provide offices and conference rooms for team projects; large meeting centres for yearly or twice-yearly "rallies" and recreation and retreat centres to encourage corporate spirit. Roving secretaries can supply some day-to-day contact."*[16]

---

[16] Faith Popcorn, 52.

## The right to be employed

One of the causes of the economic crisis in which we live is that our idea of professional life is most often tied to a notion that we have a right to be employed.

In 1974, politicians affirmed that Europe could not afford to finance 10 million jobless and that necessary steps should be taken to ensure that this situation never occurs. Currently official sources estimate there now to be some 20 million unemployed not counting those excluded from society.

Nobody takes any notice anymore of campaign slogans like "Vote for us and all your problems will be solved." Politicians are becoming more realistic. We no longer believe in false promises. Everyone needs to take charge of their own lives and not depend on the government to give them their "daily bread."

The notion of "the right to be employed" should be banished, and replaced once and for all by the "right to make a living."

Indeed, the right to be employed is not even realistic. Why should a commercial firm that is no longer making a profit continue to guarantee a job to its workers? In the short term, it avoids strikes, but in the long term, it is a disaster. It is not always the shortest route to bankruptcy, but it makes the company run a serious risk of losing any competitive edge.

If one asks employees where does the money come from that pays their salary, the majority of them will respond that it comes from the company that employs them. Other than the national banks, no company whatsoever makes their own money! The employee's salaries are financed out of the company's revenues which come from clients who buy the products and services offered. The ability to pay salaries is solely dependent on having successful product lines.

A commercial business is nothing more than a gathering of skills of a certain number of people to produce and market a service. Needs evolve constantly so companies must adapt and change. A new business is founded while others are liquidated — nothing is written in stone. Change is necessary in order to follow demand and innovation.

"Job security" and "life time employment" are an encumbrance to the necessary changes that firms must undertake to remain competitive. These ideas are detrimental to the system. They originated at the end of World War II when governments had to attract personnel competent enough to rebuild what had been destroyed. One incentive was the appointment system which guaranteed complete security.

The situation has since deteriorated. Wages of government employees are often lower than equivalent posts in the private sector so now most people entering administrative positions are doing so primarily for the job security.

The people who are the most interested in security are those who are most afraid of change. The system, therefore, has a tendency to stagnate and resist evolution without a great deal of worry. Just look at the case of legal clerks' offices in Belgian courthouses. They have no notion of computers. They work with books, sheets and red and green pencils.

Even so, employees in the private sector are still interested in ways to maximise their job security. In many cases this results in an attitude of self preservation. These employees, all too many, while being wary not to make any serious mistakes that would put their job on the line, are principally looking for a way to keep their authority.

Their personal interests match that of the company on occasion, but deviate from it all too often. Positions of power are no longer sought after in order to start up audacious projects or have brilliant ideas, more for the title, the laurel wreaths and benefits that are attached. They give it all they have got to get to the top, but, unfortunately rarely acquire a sense of interest in the common good and ethical values on the way. Too many managers remain suspended in their own personal world of self interest.

But can we blame them? Beyond the title that their job bestows upon them, bosses of large corporations, like the leaders of our countries deservedly enjoy significant financial rewards for the good work they have done.

Problems arise, however, when people without a sense of morals make it to the top motivated only by the advantages they will receive when they get there. The same phenomenon exists in the government sector. Why are political decisions not made until after elections? Because the short term-personal interests comes before the long term-general good.

Fortunately this trend is starting to reverse itself. More and more positive people with high ethical standards have begun to address the problems of a poorly guided system. We are cleaning up political practices as well as commercial ones. We are at a time when we hear about things like the "clean-hands operations" in Italy, or in Germany where former government officials are sharing their jail-cells with directors of large industrial groups.

Dynamic people no longer see any future for themselves in the large existing structures and are looking for alternatives. These truly independent people neither want to have their earnings limited nor their liberty cut short. They are moving away from the idea that remuneration must be proportional to the number of hours worked.

# Part Two

# Multi-level Marketing

*MLM yes, pyramid Selling no!*
*Pascal Clément*[1]

---

[1] French minister in charge of the relationship with the Parliement

# Chapter I
# The Evolution of Distribution

MLM has appeared as a new marketing technique and illustrates that changes this century have made it possible for the development of new ways to distribute products.

## Distribution: the opportunity of the nineties

In the past production costs have constituted 80% of the price of a product and distribution and transportation costs the other 20%. Due to the ineffectiveness of transportation there was no choice but to produce products close to their market. In those times, it was good business to look for ways to reduce production costs.

Technological innovations have permitted an extraordinary reduction in production costs. The appearance of highly-specialised machinery has lowered costs associated with labour, and production lines are increasingly automated.

The appearance of low cost transportation — most importantly train and boat, followed by truck and air —

have allowed delocalisation of production sites. It is now easy to produce all goods at lower cost in distant locations. Even when products are not entirely manufactured elsewhere, it is often the case that individual components are manufactured abroad and assembled locally.

Production costs have consistently declined since the 1950's allowing the client to buy merchandise at a significantly better price. Today's task is not simply to produce a product or service, but to reach the consumer.

The genuine wealth of an airline is not in the number or types of air planes that the company owns. The difference between a flourishing company and one on the brink of bankruptcy is the efficiency of its reservation and ticketing computer network. The ticket sold will be the one that has been accessible to the public through the largest number of selling points.

If an airline under-estimates the volume of its clients, it can always rent aircraft on a temporary basis from specialised businesses, thereby raising production. Production has become flexible and distribution has become the most important task in business today.

The American company McDonald's makes and sells hamburgers. They may not be the best hamburgers in the world, however, they are found everywhere. They are, therefore, the hamburgers that are the best sold. When McDonald's started production of its breaded chicken — "Chicken McNuggets" — McDonald's became overnight the largest seller of chicken in the world. All this is a result of the power of distribution.

For a long time, consumers looked to brand-names as an indicator of assured quality. Since the 1980's, however, large stores have begun to sell merchandise under a generic label. These stores are relying exclusively on their means of distribution to sell products. Their publicity costs have disappeared allowing them to sell products even cheaper. We now find excellent quality merchandise, and even luxury items, with a Sainsbury label in England, or a Migros label in Switzerland. This type of chain store researches what type of products are selling the best and then orders them direct from the manufacturer to market to the public at a lower price.

Distribution is one of today's largest areas of potential growth. Europe contains 350 million consumers who are waiting for quality products more often than not manufactured overseas.

*

## Distribution techniques

Since the industrial revolution in 1850, the techniques for distribution have been evolving constantly. Village markets were rivalled by small shops. Larger stores (in Britain, Harrods; in France, La Samaritaine) and chain stores (Marks & Spencers, Kaufhof) followed. Their success lead to supermarkets and warehouse stores offering similar products at more interesting prices.

At the same time two other techniques of distribution have developed: direct selling, and franchising.

## Direct selling through a representative

Consumers want to buy high quality merchandise at interesting prices with good service. Salespeople strive to satisfy them. One way of lowering distribution costs while still assuring the quality of service, is to reduce the number of middlemen in the distribution process. The wave of direct selling techniques can be divided into groups: door-to-door selling, distance selling (mail order by catalogues, telephone services, television, minitel), parties organised as product showcases and membership clubs. Overheads, such as storage and high street premises, are thereby eliminated.

Door-to-door selling has seen its glory days. In the 1930's delighted housewives bought revolutionary new vacuum cleaners from dapper young men who impressed them with the countless merits of their product. Today the same representatives would not succeed relying on the same methods. With a high percentage of working women there is not always someone home. Furthermore, we no longer open the door of our protected cocoon to someone we do not know. We fear them to be a thief, staking out the place for their next "job."

In other respects, the system of selling by commercial representative has also witnessed inefficiency costs, as defined by Ronald Coase. At the heart of the business, there are problems in the management of personnel and the respect of geographical market subdivisions. Furthermore, the salesperson, who approaches work with a great deal of dynamism, may actually be limited in his potential to expand the business by a superior who does not want to loose their own position.

**The franchise**

To avoid personnel problems, some manufacturers have developed the system of franchising. The manufacturer directs the development of a product, its publicity, and the development of the selling point, but passes on the right to conduct sales to an independent distributor. The basic principle is to promote client fidelity. The clients are assured of the quality of the goods and services that are provided to them, no matter where they are purchased.

Let's take another look at McDonald's. At its inception they sold hamburgers. When they became a franchise they not only selected the ingredient for the food they also standardised all other aspects of the business: the hats that the cashiers wear, the layout of the children's play area and everything else is the same in Montreal as it is in Bangkok.

On the other hand, the managers of most McDonald's are independents. They have bought the right to sell McDonald's hamburgers. They follow courses in the proper techniques of serving clients so that the quality of service is exactly the same everywhere. McDonald's, the franchiser, only sees a small fraction of the price of each hamburger sold, but because their stores are all over the world this adds up to a very considerable amount of money. The franchisee also stands to make considerable profit as they have an almost guaranteed success formula.

Franchise holders develop their own business by making use of a promising idea developed by the franchiser and its purchasing power.

Companies such as Hertz, Avis, Benetton, B.P., and many others bring to their franchise holders a name, a reputation, publicity, know-how, and after-sale service within a contractual time limit. To benefit the holder pays an entry fee and a proportion of their profits. The franchise holder is contractually bound to respect rules aimed at unifying commercial policies, such as the look and decoration of the selling point, the uniforms of the personnel, supplies, and the use of some publicity and promotional materials.

# Chapter II
# The Workings of MLM

MLM draws its inspiration from principles taken from both franchising and direct selling. From the franchise, it takes the principle of independent distribution carried out in close relation to the manufacturer. From direct selling, it takes the principle that there is only one intermediary between the MLM company and the consumer. The intermediary is the distributor.

By bringing together characteristics of franchising and direct selling, MLM has succeeded in avoiding their individual inconveniences. Setting up an MLM business does not require the capital that is necessary to purchase a franchise, and the selling methods of the independent distributor are very different from those of the door-to-door salespeople and travelling representatives.

The newly created role of 'distributor' is, therefore, vastly different from that of people involved in other forms of distribution.

The aim of this chapter is not to look at the details of MLM. The bibliography of this book contains a list of works that thoroughly investigate the subject. Instead, here we would like to understand the principles at work in MLM by getting to know its broader characteristics.

Peter Clothier defines MLM as follows:

*"A method of selling goods directly to consumers through a network developed by independent distributors introducing further distributors, income being generated by retail and wholesale profits supplemented by payments based upon the total sales of the group built by a distributor."*[1]

There are on one side, manufacturing firms who have turned to MLM to market their product, and on the other, people called distributors who create their own individual distribution businesses. The distributor must be introduced by another distributor — referred to as a sponsor.

In the United States, AT&T, Colgate-Palmolive, Gillette, and many other companies supply products to MLM businesses or operate MLM subsidiaries.

## Word of Mouth

Technically, MLM is the capitalisation of the principle of word of mouth. When we like a car, a hotel, a restaurant, a brand of tea or whisky, we publicise it by telling those around us. When we decide to buy a dog or a camcorder, or to go on vacation, we ask the advice of friends and listen to their recommendations with great interest.

---

[1] Peter Clothier, *Multi-level Marketing* (London: Kogan Page, 1992) 47.

Our opinions are influenced by people around us. Katz and Lazarsfeld did a study on personal influence.[2] They showed that 30% of our decisions are directly affected by it.

Most of the time, the business that benefits from this efficient word-of-mouth publicity does not even know that it is going on and can not thank those who are doing it for them. MLM companies are able to reward people who use word of mouth publicity to recommend a product that they like to others.

*"As friends share good news, when you discover a product or a service that gives you some benefit, you have a desire to tell others about it. In network marketing, this is exactly why you get paid. Think of this money as a way for the company to say 'thank you' !"*[3]

## A network of independent distributors

Each distributor in MLM has two opportunities. On the one hand, they show and recommend the product. He or she profits from a margin on the sale (the direct selling principle).

On the other hand, the distributor, for a small annual fee, is allowed to set up their own network. They profit from the turnover it generates (the franchise principle). Payment usually comes directly from the MLM company which calculates each distributors cheque with the aid of sophisticated computer systems.

---

[2] Elihy Katz and Paul F. Lazarsfeld, *Personal Influence* (New York: The Free Press, 1955) 234

[3] John Kalench, *Being the Best You Can Be in MLM* (San Diego: MIM Publications, 1988) 8

Distributors are encouraged to dedicate their time and energy equally between these two functions.

## Limited risk

It is not necessary to invest capital to create an MLM distribution business. A few demonstration products are all that is necessary to begin. Some distributors may risk keeping a small stock, but the purchase of these products is not obligatory.

## No boss, no employees

The system of MLM makes use of a form of total business independence. A small independent business is set up under the direction of one person and without subordinates. The relationship that one has with the sponsor is a relationship of equals. Those who have tried to direct the work of the members of their network have met with little success. Each distributor must take his or her own responsibility. The success of each distributor depends on their own individual work.

In MLM, there are no secretaries, jacks-of-all-trades, salespeople, or any other person to carry out the work, therefore, there are no labour-management problems or calculation of redundancy payments to undertake, nor does one have to foresee holiday pay and replacement workers.

## A family business

A popular way to conduct business for a large number of MLM distributors is to work in families. Married and non-married couples, fathers and sons, mothers and daughters, sisters and brothers have found many ways to work together. This is entirely possible in this flexible profession where no formal qualifications are necessary. Often mothers of families are delighted to be able to take part in their husbands' businesses, even if it is part-time work, they do not have to limit themselves to stuffing envelopes.

## You can not get by on your own

What is really unique to MLM is that one can not succeed without helping others to do the same. Remuneration is related to the success of the people that have been sponsored. One creates a truly profitable business when one has succeeded in helping many other people to create their own flourishing businesses.

By sponsoring one person, the distributor commits to supplying them with help and information. A new distributor needs support to learn the profession. The system of payment, as it is established, motivates the sponsor to help the distributor who has just set up shop.

## Open to everyone

MLM distributorship is open to everyone. It does not matter whether or not you have graduated from college, if you are male or female, young or old, black or white. A wide variety of people have succeeded in building MLM businesses. Former waiters, secretaries, business people, teachers, doctors, veterinarians, carpenters — all of them have had the great success that they so desired by working with the MLM system.

Even if everyone took a chance at it, not all will succeed. At the present time, in Europe only 20 to 40 % of distributors make it through their first year. Finding the first good people to sponsor is actually more difficult than it seems. Many do not properly evaluate their will to succeed. Giving up is so easy — even more so since the financial stake is limited.

Not surprisingly, there are therefore similarities between the MLM distributors that have made it work. One is a spirit of openness. Also a positive and optimistic character, a willingness to take responsibility for themselves and have clearly defined personal goals. They have a purpose in life and high self esteem. They are persistent and adventurous pioneers. They work hard and are able to help others.

**Full-time or part-time**

The number of people who work their MLM business part-time is greater than that of people who do it full-time. Many distributors are able to take advantage of the flexibility of MLM in order to manage their time as they wish and to profit from the additional income that this business provides.

It is very easy to begin your own MLM business working evenings and weekends, to keep it going in parallel to another job, then to devote all your time to it when it is fairly well developed after a year or two (sometimes more, sometimes less).

This sort of work offers a flexibility that no longer exists in our society which has been "paralysed" by its job status. The status of the student, the salaried employee, the unemployed person, the retired person. . .

\*

# Chapter III
# Ethics in MLM

In Europe, in spite of the success that it has already had, MLM has only just started to build momentum. It needs to create a good name for itself by adopting a rigorous ethical code.

The principle of MLM is highly ethical. Competition is replaced by a commitment to others. It is open to everyone, and the chance for success is equal for all. Selling is carried out without pressure.

Abuse of the system is, however, possible and must be avoided at all costs.

All distribution methods have had their share of corruption. Discount stores have been known to sell a number of products at a loss in order to attract customers and some franchisers have conducted themselves improperly with respect to their franchise holders. This has not resulted in us believing that all discount shops and franchises are unethical.

Furthermore our law-makers have stepped in to regulate new professions and to prohibit their abuse.[5]

Law always lags behind with regard to evolution of practice. It is therefore essential for the common welfare of the profession, that a code of ethics, dictated from within, is followed by MLM firms themselves and respected by each of their distributors.

Numerous professions have adopted ethical codes that they expect each practitioner of their trade to abide by. The deceptive doctor, shady lawyer, corrupt pharmacist, and dishonest notary will all be sanctioned by their professional regulatory bodies.

The MLM profession consists of groups of distributors. The personal conduct of each will have an impact on the industry's image as a whole — bad or good. Even though a "regulatory body" of MLM distributors does not yet exist in most European countries, each distributor should ensure that certain basic ethical principles are respected[6]. Such an order does already exist to a certain extent in Great Britain. . .

## The Direct Selling Association Code of Ethics

MLM's foundations lye in the principles of direct selling, therefore, it can easily adopt the same ethical code.

---

[5] The law in most European countries forbids practices that are often confused with MLM — such as «snowball» scams and «pyramid selling». The members of these networks are paid only when a new member enters the system. There are no products sold, but every one puts in a down payment hoping to be reimbursed by the entry of subsequent people into the network. These people also must pay high initial fees. The last people into the system obviously loose their shirts! The ethical code of legal MLM marketing seeks to entirely forbid its connection to these pyramid-like «snowball» systems.

[6] See Peter Clothier, *Multi-level Marketing* (London: Kogan Page, 1992) 271

Each European country has an established direct selling group, e.g. the Direct Selling Association (DSA) in Britain. These bodies are represented at a European level by the Federation of European Direct Selling Associations (FEDSA) and globally by the World Federation of Direct Selling Associations (WFDSA).

These groups have drawn up guidelines relating to ethical codes which their members must respect. Many MLM companies are already associated and have incorporated their principles into the contracts that bind them to their distributors. The dishonest distributor who breaks the rules will loose their right to do business.

These associations have laid down two categories of regulations:

– rules of good conduct to protect the consumer, including a genuine product, guarantee from the company, the availability of detailed and honest product information, and a quality service including after sales support.

– conduct of the salesperson and the company including recruitment methods, a formal written contract, minimal entry fees, good training, and a reliable supply of merchandise. . .

These general rules of the Code are applied to Multi-level Marketing, but MLM specific rules must be added to the list. Some of these rules are aimed at the company and some at the distributor.

## The company's ethical code

### Small entry fee

The company must ensure that entry fees are proportional to the real administrative or training costs involved in creating the distributorship. This participation must not benefit the sponsor in any way. The entry fee should be paid directly to the MLM company and not to the sponsor to avoid a "pyramid" or "snowball" type of business structure.

*

## No obligation to buy a stock of merchandise

The contract between the company and the distributor should clearly stipulate that there is no purchasing obligation imposed, otherwise the sponsor would generate an income purely by signing up distributors regardless of whether or not retail sales take place.

The new distributor, however, has an interest in buying demonstration products to help build their business. The difference between being "overstocked" and "well-stocked" is difficult to define and for the large part depends on the objectives of the distributor and the magnitude of the commitment made vis-à-vis the new distribution business.

The MLM company may stipulate a reasonable maximum limit of demonstration products that may be purchased. It may restrict investment for the first product order and verify that the first products have actually been sold before authorising further supplies.

*

## Obligation to buy back unsold merchandise

The company should commit contractually to buy back any merchandise that the distributor does not sell.

This complements the "no obligation to buy stock" rule. This approach does not exist in the world of traditional business where all merchants incapable of selling their goods simply take a loss, but serious MLM companies have been so successful, they can afford to build this "limited-risk" option into their contractual obligation to the distributor. Nevertheless, one must be cautious that the company is stable. If it goes bankrupt, the guarantee of buy-back will be useless!

*

**No exaggerated profit from advertising and training material (Cassettes and Brochures)**

The MLM distributor's job is so different from what we are accustomed to that a complete training program is required. Manuals, videos and audio cassettes have been designed to help circulate the correct information.

Also, MLM companies often supply distributors with informational materials about the product or about selling techniques, such as 'The Distributor's Tool-kit' or "Getting Started Packages". The sale of these tools, all very important to acquire the business knowledge, should always represent a very small part of the revenues of both distributor and companies.

*

## The distributor's ethical code

The distributor must in turn imperatively obey a few good conduct rules, the breaking of which would do harm to the entire profession.

### Honesty about the performance of a product

There is always the temptation to get carried away by one's own enthusiasm above a product. It is, however, necessary to maintain an irreproachably objective point of view and to allow consumers to form their own opinions. Enthusiasm is a great asset in MLM and necessary to succeed — however, one must remain honest!

The MLM industry, like all forms of commerce, is subject to regulations that forbids misleading advertising and deception.

Moreover, suggesting untrue product benefits creates a serious problem for the company and for other distributors as well. Word of mouth is a double-edged sword. It is great when positive information circulates rapidly, and the quality and advantages of goods or services is widely known to everyone, however, negative information can also get around with double the speed and efficiency.

\*

### Honesty about the magnitude of the work

The MLM system is almost unique in that there are genuinely no limits to the revenues that it can generate. Beyond this honest statement, the new distributor, however, needs to be aware that to establish such a prosperous business requires a considerable amount of persistent effort. There is much damage done by novice distributors who assure you that you will just have to sit back and wait for the money to roll in!

For the most part, an MLM distributor only begins to see significant returns after 2 to 5 years of work, depending on their personality, the quality of the effort they have put in, and the level of motivation of the people who make up the team.

Success requires perseverance, self-confidence, action, a positive and optimistic attitude, determination, ethics, etc. This is why the vast majority of people who think of MLM as a "get rich quick" scheme will be disappointed, and will not make it through the first year.

**Respect of legal formalities**

The MLM distributor's profession is of a commercial nature. It is not a job one is 'employed' to do, but a chance to create one's own distribution business, therefore, each country will probably have legal formalities which must be followed.

It is obvious that the MLM distributor's income is taxable and must be declared. To hide it is not only fiscal fraud, but it also tarnishes the image of the MLM industry. The sponsor who is helping a new distributor to create a business has the duty of reminding him or her of this.

Having said that, some MLM companies take charge of all or part of the administrative formalities normally carried out by a distributor. This is a great incentive and has persuaded more than one to get started. It is, however, the responsibility of each distributor to verify that all legal obligations have been fulfilled.

∗

All regulations respected, MLM will become what it was designed to be: an excellent means to do business with a very small investment and a serious possibility to anyone to begin a new profession.

These ethical rules are so important that they have drawn the attention of our law-makers. A French law has just been passed and the British Parliament is reviewing its act on the subject. Other European countries will follow. The European Parliament is also currently aware of the development of MLM and in the near future is likely to adopt a European regulation.

\*

# Part Three

# MLM and Today's Trends

*The future is not what it used to be anymore.*
Yogi Berra

# Chapter I
# MLM Conformity to Today's Trends

MLM's success is largely due to the fact that it corresponds to the major European trends.

**MLM and "The Return Home"**

MLM is a form of direct selling that takes place in the clients home - in their beloved cocoon. MLM allows for a form of simplified and pleasant buying. We have security in knowing that we are dealing with a friend who is not trying to "pull one over on us." And the pleasure of being able to profit from a warm contact without opening the door to a stranger. Quite the opposite from the traditional idea of a door-to-door salesman forcing his way in and selling things we do not even want.

*

**MLM and "The Wary Buyer"**

We buy with care. We look for good quality at a reasonable price and listen to other people's advice. What are we most sensitive to? To the power of "word of mouth", to what our friend tried out for us and what they liked. We feel comfortable buying in an atmosphere of trust, and who would we have more trust in than someone who we have known for a long time?

The MLM company supports the efforts of its distributors by setting up toll-free numbers for consumers. They can call a customer service line which is at their disposal for answering questions.

\*

### MLM and "Personalised Selling"

MLM satisfies our desire for personal service — it makes us feel special.

After sales service must be impeccable. We expect the MLM company and distributor to resolve any problems that may occur with our product once we have purchased it. The company is aware of the fact that it relies solely on the power of word of mouth advertising.

\*

### MLM and "Nature and Technology"

MLM offers a serious alternative to the crazy "race to success" for those who want to manage their own time, and create their own business without taking too many risks. We can finally work from home close to our family. Mothers can reconcile the demands of work and the education of their children.

New communication technologies are perfectly suited to the MLM distributor's needs. Telephone and fax are available to everyone. More and more people have video-players allowing them to watch cassettes presenting companies and their products. As airline tickets become more affordable, building MLM networks internationally is increasingly cost effective.

MLM companies rely on powerful computers and sophisticated programs which permit them to handle the millions of orders demanded by hundreds of thousands of distributors. It brings together the technology of tomorrow in the best way: conference call training and product upgrades are common in the US. One MLM leader speaks to anywhere between 5 and 1000 people at once. Visual conference calling in the future will make this an even more powerful tool.

\*

## MLM and "Quality of Life"

We have become our own experts and form our own opinions on numerous issues. We are aware of the fact that we are capable of acquiring new knowledge in new fields. To learn a new profession which can propel us towards success appears an enriching challenge to us. Our lack of belief in the welfare state strengthens this desire to set our own goals and find a way to achieve them.

As a result of this, many people who get involved in MLM discover that the personal development they experience helps them in many aspects of their life; more self confidence, better listening and public speaking skills and higher self esteem are often indirectly acquired as a result of distributing the product or service, and developing a network.

With hard work the result can be an exceptional income and escape from the familiar treadmill of traditional business.

*

## MLM and "The Search for Ethical Values"

Due to MLM's fundamental principles, only those who are willing to help others, improve themselves, work with a strong code of ethics and accept responsibility for their actions will reap benefits. Power hungry money grabbers will not get far as they cannot develop relationships of trust which are essential in network building.

*

# Chapter II
# MLM and New Buying and Working Habits

MLM fits the current European trends perfectly and corresponds to our new way of buying from home through personal contact and guaranteed service. It also allows more autonomous and flexible working habits.

## MLM: distribution that suits our new buying habits

Through the distribution process, MLM fulfils another very important role, customer education — about which Paul Pilzer has written.[6]

The first washing machine was introduced in 1922. It took about ten years until everyone had heard about this fabulous invention and could find a shop in which to buy it. In 1939, the first black and white televisions appeared, and after the war, new consumer items were invented with increasing frequency which have come to revolutionise our daily lives. The process of innovation has accelerated to the point where nowadays, new inventions do not show up every five years, but every six months!

---

[6] Paul Zane Pilzer and Mark and Renee Reid Yarnell, *Should You Quit Before You're Fired?* (Carson City, Nevada: Quantum Leap, 1992) 29

Large discount supermarkets have seen phenomenal success due to their ability to reduce cost by buying in bulk. They also fulfilled another fundamental role: anyone can go to a big store to buy what they want and at the same time see new inventions. This is still a way by which many people pick and choose, however, today people are happier if they can get the same quality of information without fighting through crowds!

TV and other forms of media advertising have for a long time influenced our perception of news products and services, but we no longer buy without question. It is none the less, so efficient that advertising costs have rocketed to such a degree that it is only a cost effective tool for mass-market products.

The shopper who wants more specialised information has to look elsewhere — specialised shops and publications, the advice of sales people (which is not always accurate in larger shops) and increasingly, advice from friends who are happy with the particular item they have bought.

MLM satisfies all these criteria — buying based on friendly advice received in our own homes. The distributors job changes from the role of a salesperson to that of a communicator and teacher, who develops contacts and builds rappour.

This will lead to situation where manufacturers will consider more and more the possibility of using existing networks to distribute their products.[7] What better, more rapid, efficient, and inexpensive way exists to make

---

[7] One French writer has envisioned such a phenomenon. See Jacques Masurel, *La vente multi-niveaux* (Ferney Voltaire: Interconcept, 1994) 80.

a new product known? Word of mouth is not only powerful, but it guarantees a certain level of truth by its very nature. We are taking charge of our responsibilities and we are becoming wary consumers. Trickery is no longer tolerated. A bad product or a bad service will not be recommended by thousands or even millions of individuals.

*

### The MLM industry: a work alternative

Why are MLM companies experiencing phenomenal growths during economic crisis, reduced economic growth, and frequent redundancies? How can they do this without even incurring short, middle and long term debt?

Effectively, MLM companies can minimise inefficiency costs and avoid transaction costs[4] by :

— using independent distributors who work at their own speed, for their own objectives and for their own profits. No bosses, no subordinates — no hierarchy at all in terms of traditional business — exactly the kind of system described as "Hierarchy of a Network of Contacts" by John Naisbitt.[5] These distributors are, therefore, not held under a contract of employment with all the associated costs and problems.

— minimising the number of actual employees to those who manufacture the product, arrange deliveries

---

[4] See Part One Chapter II.
[5] See John Naisbitt's *Megatrends* and *Megatrends 2000*, full citation of both above. See also Appendix 2.

and support the registration, payment, and queries of distributors.

Transaction costs, as Coase defined them, are avoided. Efficient computer systems ensure that distributors are paid according to the companies marketing plan. Also the company helps with some transaction costs (e.g. phone hot lines, organisation of opportunity meetings and trainings, product delivery, etc.). and others are absorbed by the distributors themselves who are directly bound to the company — not to each other.

Coase recommends that a professional organisation should balance inefficiency and transaction costs. This is the case in MLM so the system is stable. Due to the fact that both of these costs are minimal, the MLM method attains extraordinary results — and the industry is only now starting to gain momentum!

MLM also avoids some of the unfair situations in traditional business where two workers performing the same work are paid unequally due to seniority. Similarly, young dynamic workers do not have to wait for their boss to quit before they can get a promotion. It is unnecessary to fire elderly workers and there are no forced retirements when times are hard.

Distributors are paid on the basis of the turnover realised by their group. The company effectively pays for the team development just as much as it does for the retailing of the product. This is why there are no limits to the earnings that a distributor can make.

The opportunity to create a large group is the same for everybody — they all have the same company and the same products — the only variable is the individual and what they are prepared to put into the business. It is not uncommon for a new recruit to build a stronger business than their sponsor. As corporations decline, therefore, thousands, even millions can prosper in a new MLM professional career.

What about MLM and the argument for 'the right to be employed'? Is MLM distribution a 'real profession', or just a hobby for bored housewives looking for a way to make some extra money?

MLM is unique in that anyone can do it. There are no exams or entrance tests, and although some sponsors may only dedicate their time to high potential candidates, in general anyone who wants to join is welcomed.

The issue of whether or not it is a real job therefore arises as there is no prestige in 'being accepted' as a distributor — you do not even need an approval of a bank loan as start up costs are so low. The principle is that someone who seriously wants to create a distribution business can do it.

The flip side of the coin is that as the opportunity is open to everyone there is no guarantee of success. This is one of MLM's biggest criticisms, but there are many parallel situations which we happily accept — school for example is open to everyone but not everyone completes it successfully!

It is up to the individual to access their own abilities and working habits and decide if MLM is for them.

MLM is not a business for those who have never succeeded in any of their goals through laziness or other bad habits. In general it requires people who are (or want to become) selfconfident, persistent and of a positive frame of mind.

MLM does therefore offer the 'right to make a living' rather than the 'right to be employed'. Anyone unhappy with their situation can learn to be a successful MLM distributor.

*

# Part Four

# The Future of MLM

*Consumers and companies
have everything to gain from
this development.*

Edmond Alphandery[1]

[1] French minister of economy

MLM is the perfect distribution method to satisfy Europeans current lifestyle and habits. It is common, however, for it to come up against criticism. People may have quickly formed a negative opinion based on a bad newspaper article and believe MLM is a type of "scam".

Why is there such a difference between the excitement of distributors and the skepticism of others?

MLM is a relatively unknown marketing innovation, and is not yet, therefore, universally accepted.

This is not surprising. Society has certain ways of dealing with new ideas and change. It is interesting to see how these patterns are reflected in the reaction to MLM.

*

# Chapter I
# The Speed at which Change Occurs

It is possible that your neighbour has never called for a pizza delivery, loves to work in the infrastructure of a large corporation, enjoys the hectic life of the big city and has not, nor never will read a self-development book of psychology. Not everyone deals with the evolving world in the same way. Some are open to change and some are more confortable on holding to tradition.

### Adopting new ideas

In 1983, an American economist, Everett M. Rogers, evaluated the time necessary for consumers to accept new ideas.[1] He noted that people react differently to new products and concepts. When a successful product is launched the level of sales starts small but as more people accept innovation this grows to a peak, then declines only to be purchased by those slow to change their habits.

---

[1] Everett M. Rogers, *Diffusion of Innovations* (New York: The Free Press, 1983).

He identified five groups of consumers :

— 2.5% of consumers are pioneers and embrace innovation. They try new ideas, take risks and possess a spirit of adventure.

— 13.5% are forward thinking and adapt to changes. Their opinion is respected and they adopt the role of leaders. At the right moment they will accept new ideas, but will do so with caution.

— 34% are the majority of forward-thinkers, who like innovation, but don't have the same pioneering attitude. Their dominant characteristic is that they think deeply about their decisions.

— 34% can be referred to as the "slow majority". These are the skeptics who will only accept innovation once it is backed by the weight of public opinion.

— 16% of consumers are traditionalists and are slow to change. Their fear of change and evolution is only overcome at the point in time when the 'innovation' is so widely accepted that it has in fact become part of tradition.

*

**The psychological process of accepting change**

All of us, regardless of which group we may be in, must pass through a series of psychological phases in order to accept a new idea. What differentiates us is the speed by which we pass through the cycle. They are:

— Indifference: We pay slight attention to something in the beginning.

— Derision: We react to the innovation with a derisive smile, if not full-blown laughter.

— Opposition: We look for any good reasons to justify believing the innovation to be impossible.

— Acceptance: We finally find enough evidence to accept the new idea.

— Indispute: Hasn't that always been the case?

Consider the example of private radio broadcasting in Europe. It began in the 1970's when enthusiasts started transmitting unofficially in a 20 kilometres radius (*phase of indifference*).

These pioneering individuals, usually young, became a target of ridicule to their friends (*phase of derision*). Soon popularity grew, especially among teenagers to a point where advertisements could be introduced as a means of revenue.

The popularity gave rise to government intervention who declared the airwaves to be the property of the State and could only be assigned to "serious" radio companies. This outlawed the independents and resulted in arrests and seizure of equipment (*phase of opposition*).

In spite of this opposition the movement grew in power and ten years later the conscientious public began to accept the idea of privately held stations. Laws were adapted accordingly (*phase of acceptance*) and independant stations are now common (*phase of indispute*). Some are spectacularly successful — "Lovin' Fun" on Fun Radio in France, for example, receives up to 40,000 calls daily from young people eager to be on the air. Up to two and a half million people from several French speaking countries tune in every night via satellite.

Microwaves were at first regarded with indifference. Why have a second oven when the first one works perfectly well? There is little enough space in the kitchen, and anyway it will only be a passing fad.

Then the opposition phase. Aren't these waves dangerous? They probably cause cancer or lead to sterility. According to rumours, manufacturers of microwaves are knee-deep in legal battles in the United States! We have got to avoid the same situation in Europe at all costs!

Then more and more people realised the benefits and now microwaves are part of everybody's life. When we buy some frozen products, the microwave is the only cooking method suggested on the box.

*

## The acceleration of evolution

From the beginning of time, man has been affected by his technological innovations. The Fire Age, Stone Age, Iron Age and Industrial Age mark distinct periods of History each of which revolves around the discovery of a new technology developed over hundreds of years.

The 20th century has seen significant agricultural breakthroughs. From 1930 to 1980 the number of people employed in this industry has halved, while output has increased through the use of modern fertilisers made possible by advancement in the chemical industry.

All these changes in the space of two generations! Grandfather retires from his farm, his son works in a chemical company, and his grandson makes TVs!

For centuries it has been traditional for a son to follow in his father's footsteps. Some dynasties still exist, which produce generations of military men, lawyers, notaries, and bakers, but new professions have appeared in the last few years and changed traditions. The majority of people now work in sectors that did not exist when their parents were choosing a career.

Up to twenty years ago, starting with a large company inferred 'jobs for life'. This concept is completely alien to young people today. The economic climate and desire for variety means that the average employee will change companies every few years before maybe establishing one of their own.

One of the reasons for this is the rate at which new technological advance take place.

*"Technology is developing at an ever-accelerating rate of speed, with each new technology compounding the speed and capabilities of those that came before."*[6]

We live in an era of abounding discoveries. Alvin Toffler emphasises the rapidity of the rhythm of invention and the use and diffusion of technological break-through.[7] The more that ideas germinate in the mind of researchers, the less time separates the idea from its realisation in the form of a product. According to Toffler, if we considered all the inventors that have ever lived, 90% of them are from this generation. It seems that there is no longer a limit to the rate at which new goods and services appear.

---

[6] John Naisbitt, *Global Paradox* (London: Nicholas Brealey Publishing 1995).
[7] Alvin Toffler, *The Third Wave*, (London: Pan Books 1980).

In this time of boiling creation, it is no wonder that we are changing our professional direction many times during the course of our lives. Another result of these changes is that we no longer use most of what we learned in school. Who can tell if our own skills will still be marketable in five years time?

People can change paths to be wherever they want. It is not abnormal now for a qualified dietitian to become the director of a sporting-goods store or a registered veterinarian can become a weather forecaster on television if they really want to! The 1994 Rally champion was a former ambulance driver, Arnold Schwarzenegger became an actor after having studied chemistry and Ronald Reagan was elected president of the United States after being a film star.

*

**Resistance to change**

People have throughout history been reluctant to accept change. In the 1850's, during the industrial revolution, machines took over the job of craftsmen, farmers and many others. Weaving machines successfully increased productivity and improved quality to produce a more regular, strong fabric — and it was quicker.

Thousands of weavers lost their jobs and revolted, destroying factories and burning warehouses. They saw machines as enemies. The frightened working class perceived that the purchase of these great innovations was a personal attack on their livelihood. People went without work for some time, however, the most industrious learned how to work with the new machines. They became skilled labourers, and their lifestyle improved. In only a few years, the quality of life improved for everyone with a return to full employment.

Today the information age is having the same effect. The application of technology once again is increasing productivity. Although we have the impression that computers are replacing humans in professional occupations we will eventually witness the same trend as in the past. After the fluctuations of change have settled the result will be an improved standard of living for everyone.

As in the industrial revolution when pioneering individuals built solid businesses as a result of their investment in new machinery, it is the people who embrace new technologies today who will become highly successful tomorrow.

These technological advances also give us much more freedom than we have had in the past. We can be contacted anywhere by phone or fax and information can easily be stored and managed by computer. Now more than at any time in the past we can continue to be professionals while living outside big cities. Who likes spending three hours a day in the car going to and from work? Cities are a perfect example of lost energy and talent, culminating in dysfunctional and disorderly lives for millions.

*

**Fear of loss**

What often holds us back most from risking the unknown is the fear of losing what we already have.

This is just as true for large corporations and

governments as it is for the individual. In fact, governments spend billions of pounds supporting industries which are no longer relevant to todays markets, e.g. coal mines, steel works, and shipyards.

The money is spent keeping these industries afloat, not trying to help them or others to innovate. With a little more imagination European industry could be witnessing the same kind of technical innovations as the United States and Asia.

For the unemployed, the fear of loosing benefits greatly reduces the likelihood of them setting up their own small business. For the employed, the fear of quitting their job before they lose it may result in missed opportunities. To learn to overcome these obstacles it is therefore of primarily importance to be self-confident enough to take the risky options regardless of fears, and as a result become much better at overcoming obstacles.

*

**The pessimism of the media**

Over the course of the twentieth century, the media have become so prominent that it is now commonly known as 'the Fourth Power.'

What do we see when we read the headlines? What are the captions on televised news programs? Catastrophes, redundancies, attacks, etc.

The media like all industries must adhere to the laws of supply and demand. Journalists and newscasters alike have a legitimate concern about how many people their work is reaching. Journalists want to please their clients with high circulations, which in turn mean better revenues, and higher wages.

Obviously, therefore, it is the work of a journalist to find stories that please the public, and in our society, hot news is about catastrophes, scandals, and things that are going wrong.

Economic life regularly takes its broad themes from those that we hold dear: redundancy of workers, the bankruptcy of companies, the high rate of unemployment.[8]

But do we ever hear about workers who find a new job within a month of being fired? More emphasis is placed on the company that goes bust than the company who creates new jobs. If we believed the media, we might imagine our countries economy is in a state of catastrophe. In actual fact the great majority of us do have a roof over our heads, something to eat, and even more. Our quality of life is probably much superior to what our grandparents could ever have experienced.

Of course there are homeless whose misfortune is highlighted by the press every time the nights get colder, but have you ever seen an article on the former homeless who have found a home and the means to get by? These people have gone through bad times but made it out the other side.

A French sociologist eloquently wrote:

*"We always talk about crisis, when we live in a time of richness. In this time of richness, dramatic things*

---

[8] Janet Bodnar, *"How TV Sees the Economy"*, Changing Times December 1989: 89.

*happen. But should we dramatise them? The media has no educative role, since they prefer to dramatise things."*[9]

Good news does not excite the public with the same fascination as bad news!

\*

---

[9] Gaston Jouffroy, "*Du producteur-consommateur au citoyen,*" *Construire le travail de demain*, Editions d'organisation, Paris, 1995).

# Chapter II
# MLM as an Innovation

MLM is different from anything we currently know. To understand and embrace it, we must pass through each of the classical phases for the acceptance of innovation discussed above.

After some indifference, negative questions come to mind. "Isn't this a is sort of snowball scam or an illegal pyramid? Didn't the nightly news do a report on the similarities between MLM companies and sects? Won't I loose both my money and my friends?"

**Towards a healthy ethical code**

These questions are completely justified if the system's ethical code have not been adhered to. If we have bought a large stock of products and are not able to sell or return them to the company, we loose our money. If we try to pawn them off by harassing our friends, we risk losing them too. If our sponsor has enticed us by promising unrealistic profits in the first month by finding five other people to sign a piece of paper, we will see in time that this is all delusion.

When first introduced the franchise system was also sharply criticised. Some abuse of the system, mostly by a small minority of franchisers, sowed doubt in the minds of the public. "Wasn't it scandalous to profit from the poor gullible franchise holders?" Franchising only started to gain popularity once a strong ethical code was adopted by the entire profession.

Serious MLM companies already incorporate such ethical codes in their distributor's contracts.

Once these rules are seen to be in place and effective, MLM can begin to move from the phase of opposition to the phase of acceptance.

\*

## MLM distributor: a new profession

MLM has existed since the 1940's[7], but has only begun to gain in popularity in Europe since the 1980's.

This can partially be explained by MLM's dependance on technology. Just as Leonardo Da Vinci could not develop the flying machine he invented lacking a power source, not to be invented for centuries, neither could MLM flourish until the computer age could support its administration.

New technologies permit our society to evolve and new professions are created everyday.

It is not necessary to have studied MLM in a busi-

---

[7] For a history of MLM see Peter Clothier, *Multi-level Marketing* (London: Kogan Page, 1992) 24.

ness school or in a department of economics to create a successful distribution network. In fact most European business courses do not even include MLM in their syllabuses.[8] Schools in the United States, however, have begun to introduce course material on the subject.

MLM distributors are from all walks of life, all professions, and have an equal chance of success. Everything that needs to be known can be learned by the new distributor, and in time passed to future new recruits. In this way information and skills can be duplicated down through a network.

Professional salespeople also must learn new skills as they are often the people who have most difficulty adapting to the MLM mind-set. Door-to-door selling tricks bring disastrous results when applied to MLM. Information passed by 'word-of-mouth' transmits negative opinions as well. A sponsor has the responsibility to help a new distributor make sales by sharing the product as one shares happy experiences. The industry's image depends upon it.

*

## MLM and the process of acceptance

The third phase of the acceptance process is that of opposition. It is not surprising, therefore, that some people cry "scandal" as soon as they hear about MLM.

When first introduced in Europe, overnight mail services (Federal Express, DHL, etc.) were thought to be scandalous. They were declared illegal because they challenged the monopoly of government mail services.

---

[8] The University of Neufchatel, Switzerland, has begun to give courses on the subject.

Then people started to realise that replacing a monopoly with competition benefits both the company and the client who is assured of a better service for the price. Hundreds of new jobs were created, and express couriers are now well accepted.

Lobbies against MLM have been established by individuals and companies whose businesses will be affected by its success. The MLM approach to marketing challenges the classical method of selling and advertising. People involved in traditional distribution are frightened of loosing some of their power.

Would it nevertheless mean that MLM is harmful to society on the whole? What if MLM offers a solution to the economic crisis by offering a business whose full potential is yet to be realised?

*

## MLM and the fear of loss

Entrepreneurship frequently involves taking risks. Often this means financial risk, but can also lead to lost time and energy if there are no results. In every case, however, regardless of the end result one will always gain something from the experience - knowledge, better understanding of ourselves and others, etc.

As MLM only involves minimal financial risk and it does not force us to give up our regular job we can devote to it the time we choose.

The real risk involved in MLM is finding out whether or not we have got what it takes to succeed. It is a profession very different from any other, so it doesn't matter how many letters we have after our name — we still have to start from scratch to learn the business, and be on a equal footing with other distributors. We risk being compared to others, and being rewarded only for our results. Not everyone can stretch their "comfort zone" and do what it takes to completely overcome their limiting beliefs.

This is yet one more reason why MLM is such an opportunity! Those who feel capable of succeeding have everything within their grasp.

\*

## MLM seen through the pessimism of the media

Why do journalists only report the negative aspects of this flourishing industry? Why do they put the public on guard against products of excellent quality?

Journalists address themselves to their audience. Who is their audience? For the most part it is made up of the group of slow adaptors and cautious people. They are delighted to have their fears confirmed "in writing."

The "phase of opposition" against MLM is almost at an end in the United States and the media are beginning to praise this new industry. A franchise and MLM magazine, *Money Makers Monthly*, attracts an increasingly wide readership.

MLM in Europe is still between the phases of opposition and acceptance varying slightly from country to country, but there is no doubt that it will come into the main stream in the coming years in all European countries regardless of cultural differences.

# Conclusion

Faith Popcorn states that in order to be successful, an enterprise or idea must sooner or later satisfy four of the broad trends of American life.

MLM undeniably corresponds to all the trends currently establishing themselves in Europe. Trends usually last a minimum of ten years which leads one to believe that by the year 2005, MLM will develop here in the same way as it has so successfully in the United States and Japan.

There are today only about 500,000 Europeans involved in this system.[1] How many will be involved in five or ten years time?

MLM, as powerful as it is, can only be effective when it offers goods and services which correspond to consumer demand. Considering the increasing frequency of innovation and the growing popularity and success of MLM, there is a very good chance that by the year 2005

---

[1] As opposed to some 5,000,000 Americans.

manufactures will look more and more to this distribution method to bring their products to the market.

The new technologies of tomorrow promise to enhance the efficiency of the MLM system. Conference calls will allow us to organise opportunity meetings and trainings more easily than is currently possible.

The use of catalogues will allow MLM to evolve into a marketing technique where the distributors only role is to make recommendations and answer questions. They will simply suggest one of the catalogue's products that they have personally liked, give a demonstration, and then the client themselves can order directly by telephone, fax, mail, or even Internet!

TV home shopping, which is rapidly expanding in the United States, Japan and to a certain extent in Italy will also use the MLM's recommending technique. The TV will give the visual information necessary for the client to make a decision, and all this will be supported by the friendly distributor who sits close by.

The world is in a state of accelerated evolution. New opportunities arise everyday. MLM is one of them. It is not *the* solution to all of society's problems — unemployment, stress, conflicts of home and in the offices — but it is *one* solution, and it has the advantage of being well within the grasp of anyone who wants it.

MLM is set to succeed in Europe!

\*

# Appendix 1

# Trends identified by Faith Popcorn's Company Brainreserve

1. Cocooning or Burrowing. This is the need to protect oneself from the harsh, unpredictable realities of the outside world.

2. Cashing Out. Working women or men, questioning personal/career satisfaction or goals, opt for simpler living.

3. Down-Aging. Nostalgic for their carefree childhood, baby boomers find comfort in familiar pursuits and products of their youth.

4. Egonomics. The sterile computer era breeds the desire to make a personal statement.

5. Fantasy Adventure. Modern age whets our desire for roads untaken.

6. 99 Lives. Too fast a pace, too little time, causes societal schizophrenia and forces us to assume multiple roles and adapt easily.

7. S.O.S. (Save our Society). The country rediscovers a social conscience of ethics, passion and compassion.

8. Small Indulgences. Stressed-out consumers want to indulge in affordable luxuries and seek ways to reward themselves.

9. Staying Alive. Awareness that good health extends longevity leads to new way of life.

10. The Vigilante Consumer. The consumer manipulates marketers and the marketplace through pressure, protest, and politics.

\*

# Appendix 2

# The Ten Megatrends According to the John Naisbitt Group

In 1982 Naisbitt identified the following trends in his first book *Megatrends*:

1. From an industrial society to an informational society.
2. From a technological base to selective, high technology
3. From domestic economics to planetary economics
4. From short term to long term
5. From centralization to decentralization
6. From assistance to the individual's making it on his own
7. From democratic representation to democratic participation
8. From hierarchy to networking
9. From North to South
10. From yes-no decisions to multiple choice

In his second work, *Megatrends 2000*, he notes the following:

1. The global economy
2. Renaissance of the arts
3. Liberal socialism
4. Global lifestyle and cultural nationalism
5. Privatization of the public sector
6. Emergence of peaceful zones
7. Arrival of the power of women
8. Biologic age
9. Religious renewal
10. Triumph of the individual

\*

# Appendix 3
# Changes according to Denis Weatley

Yesterday natural resources defined power.
Today knowledge is power.

Yesterday hierarchy was the model.
Today synergy is the mandate.

Yesterday leaders commanded and controlled.
Today leaders empower and coach.

Yesterday leaders were warriors.
Today leaders are facilitators.

Yesterday leaders demanded respect.
Today leaders encourage self-respect.

Yesterday shareholders came first.
Today customers come first.

Yesterday managers directed.
Today managers delegate.

Yesterday supervisors flourished.
Today supervisors vanish.

Yesterday employees took orders.
Today teams make decisions.

Yesterday seniority signified status.
Today creativity drives process.

Yesterday production determined availability.
Today quality determines demand.

Yesterday value was extra.
Today value is everything.

Yesterday everyone was a competitor.
Today everyone is a customer.

Yesterday profits were earned through expediency.
Today profits are earned with integrity.

*

# Further Readings

Berger, Jon (1991) *The Manual of Multi-level Selling Law*, Skilfu Publishing, Farnham

Bodnar, Janet (1989) "How TV Sees the Economy", *Changing Times*, December 89

Centre des Jeunes Dirigeants (1995) *Construire le travail de demain*, Editions d'organisation, Paris

Cheung, Steven (1987) "Ronald Harry Coase", *The new Palgrave: A Dictionary of Economics*, Macmillian Press Limited, London

Clothier, Peter (1992) *Multi-level Marketing,* Kogan Page, London

Conn, Charles Paul (1985) *Promises to keep*, Berkley Books, New York

Engelhart, W. H. Prof. Dr. (1992) *Definition and Volume of Direct Selling of Goods and Services to Consumers*, Research Study of Ruhr University of Bochum, Germany, unpublished

Failla, Don (1984) *Ten Napkins Presentation*, Joe Chardwick, USA

Hitching, Francis (1993) *Boom Business of the Nineties*, MPG Publications, Manchester

Kalench, John (1988) *Being the Best You Can Be in MLM*, MIM Publications, San Diego

Katz, Elihy & Lazarfeld, Paul F. (1955) *Personal Influence*, The Free Press, New York

Kotler, Philip & Dubois, Bernard (1994) *Marketing Management*, Publi Union, Paris

Masurel, Jacques (1994) *La vente multi-niveaux*, Inter Concept, Fernay Voltaire

Naisbitt, John (1982) *Megatrends*, Warner, New York

Naisbitt, John, & Aburdene, Patricia (1990) *Megatrends 2000*, Avon Books, New York

Naisbitt, John (1995) *Global Paradox*, Nicholas Brealey Publishing, London

Nichol, Malcolm J (1989) *The Network Strategy*, Uni-Vite Nutrition Ltd, Aston Clinton

Pilzer, Paul Zane & Reid Yarnell Mark & Renee (1992) *Should You Quit Before You're Fired*, Quantum Leap, Carson City

Pilzer, Paul Zane (1991) *Unlimited Power-The Theory and Practice of Economic Alchemy*, Crown Publishers

Popcorn, Faith (1991) *The Popcorn Report*, Arrow Books Ltd, London

Rogers, Everett (1983) *Diffusion of Innovations*, The Free Press, New York
Schreiter, Tom (1985) *Big Al Tells All*, Kass Publishing, Houston

Toffler, Alvin (1980) *The Third Wave*, Pan Books, London

Toffler, Alvin (1990) *Powership*, Bantam Books, New York

Toffler, Alvin and Heidi (1994) *Creating a new Civilisation, the politics of the Third wave,* Prayers and Freedom Fondation, Washington, Atlanta

Waitley Denis (1995) *Empires of the Mind*, Nicholas Breatley Publishing, London

# Table of contents

Preface

Multi-level Marketing Short term fad or long term trend?

**Part One : What does the future hold** .............................. 13

**Chapter 1: Knowing the Trends of Tomorrow** ................. 15

The nineties
The First Trend : The Return Home
The Second Trend: The Wary Buyer
The Third Trend: Personalised Selling
The Fourth Trend: Nature and Technology
The Fith Trend: The Quality of Life
The Sixth Trend: A search for Ethics

**Chapter II : The Consequences of These Trends** ............. 27

New buying habits
Non store retailing
Direct selling
Mail order
TV home shopping
Multi-level Marketing
The new working habits
The right to be employed

**Part Two: Multi-level Maketing** .......................................... 41

**Chapter I: The Evolution of Distribution** ......................... 42

Distribution the opportunity of the nineties
Distribution technics

Direct selling through a representative
The franchise

**Chapter II**
   **The working of MLM** .................................................... 49

Word of mouth
A network of independent distributors
Limited risk
No boss, no employees
A family business
You can not get by on your own
Open to everyone
Full-time or part-time

**Chapter III: Ethics in MLM** ............................................. 53

The Direct Sellings Association Code of Ethics
The company's ethical code
Small entry fee
No obligation to buy a stock of merchandise
Obligations to buy back unsolded merchandise
No exaggerated profit from advertising
   and training material (cassettes and brochures)
The distributor's ethical code
Honesty about the performance of a product
Honesty about the magnitude of the work
Respect of legal formalities

**Part Three: MLM and Today's Trends** ........................... 61

**Chapter I: MLM Conformity to Today's Trends** ............ 63

MLM and "The Return Home"
MLM and "The Wary Buyer"
MLM and "Personalised Selling"
MLM and "Nature and Technology"
MLM and "Quality of Life"
MLM and "The Search for Ethical Values"

**Chapter II: MLM and New Buying
and Working Habits** ............................................................... 67

MLM: distribution that suits our new buying habits
The MLM industry: a work alternative

**Part Four: The Future of MLM** ........................................... 73

**Chapter I: The Speed at wich Change Occurs** ................. 77

Adopting new ideas
The psychological process of accepting change
The acceleration of evolution
Resistance to change
Fear of loss
The pessimism of the media

**Chapter II: MLM as an Innovation** ..................................... 87

Towards a healthy ethical code
MLM distributor: a new profession
MLM and the process of acceptance
MLM and the fear of loss
MLM seen through the pessimism of the media

**Conclusion** ............................................................................... 93

**Appendix 1: Trends identified by Faith Popcorn's
company Brainreserve** ........................................................ 95

**Appendix 2: The Ten Megatrends According
to the John Naisbitt Group** ................................................ 97

**Appendix 3: Changes according
to Denis Waitley** .................................................................. 99

**Further Readings** ................................................................ 101